FLABBY RABBIT

BY JOANNE M. WEBER

ILLUSTRATED BY KENDRA W. GRATTON

Print information available on the last page

Rev. date: 12/19/2017

To order additional copies of this book, contact:
Xlibris
1-888-795-4274
www.Xlibris.com
Orders@Xlibris.com

DEDICATION

I would like to dedicate this book to my family...my husband Ken, who worked tirelessly on the computer for this project. Thanks Hon, I know that letting your wife and daughter make decisions was hard sometimes, but you did it! I never knew that THE END could look so charming...good design! It was fun to have you so proud of your wife and daughter. We surely had some laughs in the process. THANKS SO VERY MUCH, HON!

My daughter Kendra also worked many long hours on the illustrations. I am amazed with her talent and her vision as well. Kendra, I loved working with you. The hours we spent were definitely one of the biggest gifts of the book for me. I am so proud of you and I am happy we have several books ahead of us. Kendra's husband Tim willingly dedicated the time Kendra needed to work on Flabby. THANKS SO MUCH, KENDRA AND TIM.

Our other children and their spouses also cheered on the process of getting Flabby into print. So to Kurt and Nancy, Chris and Laura, Kev and Maggie, and Craig and Eva, merci! For all the timely "How is Flabby coming?", the suggestions on layout or computer needs, and the joy as you heard we were progressing. I LOVE YOU DEARLY, FAMILY! THANK YOU !

Then there are friends and family who also were my cheerleaders, always hoping for the best, ordering books before they are even in print yet, and being just plain gracious and encouraging. MANY MANY THANKS.

And of course the grandkids get my special thanks..Bailey, Tristan, Gus, Brian, Jenni, Ellen, Eric, Aaron, Damian, Cameron and Colton. You make my life full and rich. You make my heart sing. You know that I see artistic talent in each of you, don't you? Keep it up, art is a very important part of life. THANK YOU, DEAR GRANDKIDS! THIS NANA LOVES YOU VERY VERY MUCH. I HOPE YOU AND YOUR CHILDREN LOVE FLABBY AS MUCH AS I LOVED WRITING IT FOR YOUR PARENTS MANY YEARS AGO.

FLABBY RABBIT

By Joanne M. Weber

Illustrated by Kendra W. Gratton

Flabby Rabbit and Squinty Squirrel were eating by the brook,
Squinty found the dinner, Flabby was the cook.
Roasted nuts and boiled greens made a tasty meal.
(Squinty asked the farmer first, for squirrels **never** steal!)

They settled down beneath the tree to take a friendly snooze
and turned their small transistor on to hear the daily news.
They felt so good, they felt relaxed, they said, "Oh this is fun!"
They stretched their tiny toesies out to toast them in the sun.

Millie Robin, Flabby's friend, had laid four eggs of blue.
She asked her buddy Flabby to watch them while she flew.
"Of course!" she said, "I'll guard them well, they're very safe with me.
I'll watch your eggs 'til you return, I'll stay beneath this tree."

But unbeknown by these two friends, Will Weasel, white and neat
Was crouched behind a glassy glen a'lookin' for a treat.
He licked his greedy drooling chops, "Those eggs are just the thing!
If I can steal those eggs for lunch, I'll be the weasel King."

Buster Bluejay stood nearby atop a towering pine.
He called a warning to his friends, "THINGS DO NOT LOOK FINE.
YOU'D BEST LEAVE NOW, THERE'S DANGER NEAR,
     A WEASEL WANTS THE EGGS,

SO TAKE OFF NOW AT HIGHEST SPEED UPON YOUR SKINNY LEGS!"

Squinty scrambled up the tree and grabbed that precious nest,
giving it to Flabby, who hugged it to her chest.
She hopped so fast into her hole and slammed her sturdy door,
Then put her dear friend Millie's nest down gently on the floor.

The eggs were fine; one two three four, and not a dent or crack.
She knew the Mama Robin would soon be coming back.

Squinty peeked outside the hole, no weasel was in sight.
Buster's screech had scared him off, it caused an AWFUL FRIGHT!

So Flabby took the precious eggs and scrambled 'neath the tree,
and Squinty put them on the branch with paws so tenderly.
Their hearts felt good, they saved the eggs, they did it for their friend,
But little did they know, these two, just how this day would end.

A noise was heard up in the nest, a crackly crunching sound.
They wondered what was happening and who had come around?
They stood up quickly, grabbing sticks, preparing for a fight.
They **had** to save dear Millie's eggs, they **had to do it Right**!

They scratched their furry little heads and said,
    "WHAT SHOULD WE DO?"
They felt them dropping on their heads,
    those eggs of purest blue.

But not the eggs themselves, you see, but SHELLS were raining down
from newly hatching BABY BIRDS up high above the ground!

"Oh boy!" said Flab. "It's Millie's babies, cute as they can be."
"Come on!" said Squinty, scrambling up the towering waving tree.

"What can we do, how can we help,
    whatever do they eat?"
Flabby said, "I think it's worms and bugs and grass,
    and maybe something sweet."

They caught a fly with Squinty's tail.
They tried some carrot pie.
But baby birdies closed their beaks.
They wouldn't even try.

Flabby had a good idea,
    and whispered to her friend,
"If we can get their Mommy back,
    this hunger strike would end."

Buster Bluejay once again screeched loudly to be heard.
He asked the forest animals to find the Mama bird.

Millie, flying high above, received the message loudly.

Taking off, she ZOOOOOMED straight home... and hugged her babies proudly!

How she thanked her dearest friends
　　who helped to guard her nest.
She gave them gifts of blackberries
　　in an antique pinewood chest.

She set about to feed her chicks a whistlin' through the trees,
while Flabby Rabbit and Squinty Squirrel
　　went home to take their ease.

The day was waRM, the suN was hot,
    and things had tuRNed out Right.
So Flabby Rabbit and Squinty SquiRReL
    got Ready foR the Night.

They put their tiny jammies on, they had a cup of
tea.

Then with
a sigh
a prayer
a song,
They went to bed,
Like me.

Printed in the United States
By Bookmasters